Keepers of the House

Max Heinegg

LILY POETRY REVIEW BOOKS

Published by Lily Poetry Review Books
223 Winter Street
Whitman, MA 02382

https://lilypoetryreview.blog/

ISBN: 978-1-957755-48-9

Library of Congress Control Number: 2024945761

Cover art: John Gallaher, *Green and Yellow,* digital art

Table of Contents

As One Does

When the door slammed, I laughed at the ghost.
When they bled on the chairs, I wet the cloth.
When they fainted, I found the nurse.
When they vomited, I asked the janitor.
When they were dumped, I let them doze.
When they failed, I taught them again.
When they cheated, we met in the hall.
When they fought, I stood between.
When they cursed, I said, *Pick your spot.*
When we rehearsed guns, I kept shit light.
When their parents died, I joined the queue.
When their siblings died, I guarded them.
When they overdosed, I wrote elegies.
When the towers fell, I lied.

For the Student Who Slept Through the Lesson on 9/11

History is the smoke
of the towers as the boy's
head rests in peace
on the desk asleep,
allowed. I know
he works all night
& just yesterday borrowed *The Iliad*
because his father *made him read The Odyssey,*
& though I'd roused him, he sleeps
again while the man falls,
an arrow, whose photographer saw, *bisecting*
the two buildings,
one where a high school friend died,
the other where my cousin worked & was on vacation from.
I wonder if this is what it means to teach
in the empire where soon there will be no
longer recognition
of fault or anger
waking him for the clip of Osama
who explains what will happen if America aims at Mecca & Medina,
& the flashback ends. The class is reminded
what Mecca means,
& the child who works to help feed his family has to
be told he's missed the bell, that he was dreaming,
perhaps of places he wants to visit,
things he wants to happen in America.

Dreamer

For _____

She doesn't want to write "the Immigration essay,"
says she can't remember Governador Valadares.
She attended the local elementary, only learning
what she was when she couldn't work. Then it made sense:
her father praying when a cop followed his pickup,
her mother cleaning because she could without a card.

She wants to write about DACA, Trump stealing
her dream of staying, going to Berklee, becoming
a musician & then, a teacher. *Like you did.*
I'm afraid she should hide her history, leave
no paper trail. Now, my help endangers her.

She decides to redact nothing, not because I've taught her
God is in the details, but because she knows
there is nothing illegal about her. At home,
my daughters walk from their bus together.
There are raids one town over. I want them to know
what the country is becoming, what it's not worth.

Sophia

I tell her Anglo-Saxon riddles
where a field may be the ocean,
a ship cries on land,
& birth is a bellows.

I guard her answers from boys
who scoff at learning & will not
meet her eyes,
but do not mind her
flowering, wreathed
in a pashmina hijab.

She knows it's easy for me to curse
my country from a lectern,
beneath a flag that allows me
to be said against it—
her family escaped Assad.

When we read how Grendel
comes out of the marsh-mist,
a terrorist
who butchers the Danes
by the hearth where they sleep,
she breathes,
That's a fire I have seen.

Michael

Feels Othello, senses Iago's schemes,
how whiteness is birthright

to say, *Demand me nothing.*
What you know, you know.

He knows, *they smile who win,* but
doesn't write his name on my quiz.

Another day, when we talk Baltimore, says,
I expect to be shot; I'm just not sure when.

Says, *College isn't happening.* With his grades,
varsity neither. Hoops at Dugger Park

where I coach girls' tennis. Waves,
doesn't mind I'm failing him. I tell myself,

no savior. Worse, I've taught the hunter
who drives patrol in the Heights

where he walks the hour of risk
the way Michael Brown once did with a friend,

living where body cameras shutter,
& the God-fearing plant guns under

the same young men teachers eager to signal
virtue try to get to enter class discussion, but

failing, watch his hands reach for his hood,
a helmet secured that dims the world,

shading the auspices of his eyes.

JiM "80"

How many classes did it take to title the year?
Gouging capitals into the fiberboard desk
while classmates endured *Gawain*; he carved
a quarter-inch deep. Assumed note-taking,
or annexed in the back row with other disruptions,
the teacher lenient or tending other fires

in the low light of this cave as it was millennia ago
in Chauvet, exhausted by a long-winded elder
recounting hunts the boy wasn't invited on yet,
the sorting of bones, hierarchies. He eased off
in the quiet of the chamber, scraping, engraving
the canvas to show he was there.

Meadow Glen Mall

The kids say *Ghetto Glen* & tag themselves,
but who having stood here & walked inside
the artless stone would not also sing
that absence of pretense is attractive dress?

Old Italian men, their working suns set
out on the ice like Inuits, take perpetual last coffees
together. Their talk familiar to me as the Irish
names in my September rankbook, families

who walk to Kohl's from one-dollar houses,
grandmother still on the first floor, to cross
Riverside Ave, & from the Heights, Brazilians
in impossible jeans wander to be seen.

On weekends, teens bore their way into the sugary
Chinese of Panda Village; in IParty, teen clerks tie
balloons I've stuffed into the bubbling trunk.
I see ex-students: Renata, who floored the boys

but stood aloof, & Thomas, the Dominican,
whose luminous eyes learned me by the third day.
In Sunday best, the Haitians' queue to Old Country
Buffet flows out the door, every daughter a Saint.

A Child Says, *Morning*

Too young for instruction, she must have heard
so many say it, ritually, so she
amplified her breath to address,
& it's not the revelation that she could
have said *Bonjou, bom dia,* or *buenos días.*

More than the beautiful variation, it's the pure
exhalation of what could have been anything.
She could have said anything,
& it would have been a good envelope
for the spirit she opened.

Legend

Aras was eleven, easily
six-feet-tall with a mustache
I marveled at. Lunchtime, he sat
with us, sipping at the red Thermos
his mother had filled. I passed
six Catholic school seasons in social exile,
plotting access, while Aras drank
calm as Madame Lloyd's displeasure
at our failures *en Francais.*

When I was called down for writing curses
in a yearbook, Aras did not blink.
When one of the headmaster's whining sons
was yanked from class for throwing a ninja star
that stuck in the other's chubby thigh,
Aras did not smirk. When the dating began,
the Izod collars popped, or
when Springsteen became faith, Aras was unmoved.

One day he was demanded from Mr. Sacca's
religion class, where scripture was assumed
culture, where Derek carved at the desk
in a full suit, fingers smeared with ink,
& I sat waiting for each bell to bless.

Aras, the word passed, had been drinking
beer. The teachers had been too far from
his breathing to recognize. His silence
had been expected & then preferred.

The drink had rested between us
the whole time, forbidden, customary.

Advisory

In what we once called homeroom, Jeremy asks
if he may get some water. *Why not?*
On his return, he tells me about his sore knee.
When I ask where the pain is, he hikes his slacks.
It's around the joint. What should I do?

He's on a plan that one of us doesn't know
the details of. I tell him, *Relax,*
we still have time before the bell,
but the nurse should see him.
That's what she's here for.

You see me, right?
Yes, I say, *I am looking at you,*
& we're talking to each other, as we do.
Don't worry, I won't mark you absent.

Lockdown

For Joe Bowen, custodian

I tell the kids, *Stay calm,* & lock the door,
find the red card to hang in the window
if need be & check for a path
to a gunless room—then direct them
to the corner by the bookshelf.

They sit on their hands, some girls on each other's laps,
spines close, all arms & shins—boys,
nearer to beauty than some will ever be
again. One will ask for music, one will ask to text
their mother, one will without asking. One will want
to & not. Together, close as empty desks. Kids
who trust that though I haven't learned all their names
yet, I would block the door for them.

On Hearing the Bomb Threat Was
Not Intended for Us

Before the robocall, the mothers were blowing up
my wife's phone via group texts. My daughter says,
nbd, they killed a school on my birthday last year.
My teacher buddy texts, *Guess I'll go, after I drop the one-year-old*
on the floor below. Part of me thinking it's a ruse to get us
to the pep rally, to find us where we have to be.

Then, I wonder if the kid who loves knives
& shoots televisions with his dad will come strapped
to blast us. No, because I know him. Or
the one who draws blood on his notebook? No,
his mood's a passing shadow. It's the kid I don't know,
who sees us as what's forcing him.

Really, I don't believe these kids would, but
my wife may be right when she reminds me of Boston,
how an improvised pressure cooker can fire nails that pierce
just fine. Will the new superintendent ensure our children are safe
when the last one ducked the spotlight, kept the bullet casings
they found in our theater from the cops who decide

the level of the threat. If it's low, they won't tell us
we might die by our standing desks, staving off slow
death. But not today. Today, we are allowed to know
we are safe, that the chat room was mistaken.
It's five miles away, one town over.
We don't need to worry about it any longer.

The Bodhisattva of Compassion

1.
Though shade rests on the branch
        of her sister & the trunk
of her mother, she looks only for the tall flower

of friendship in the garden of strangers
        where the rocky soil splits, harbors
bee-balm, wild mint, columbine.

None to assist me in the weathering
        away, Boston's three modes: cloud
fickle, *wicked* sun, & *bullshit*.

2.
I rouse my phone again, hoping for my own
        acceptance, but it's blind feelers
& the clamor of first-world problems:

broken front step bricks to stagger
        litigious mailmen, lurching Halloween
children. The house as body frames the narrative

of alignment: as around, so within,
        the basement's disused weights,
each muscle waiting on maintenance.

3.
We weave to the museum with the genius of satellites,
        road by road we avoid dukkha.
By the Rose Garden, spy the fens that shield the flesh

& its brevities, the courts where I could scarcely gather
        a rebound, across the small pond & bridge.
Six summers I taught *The Dark Thirty* & myths to the class

of Dorchester & Roxbury, welcome as water
	despite my whiteness. We shared the respite,
turning pages whose music few depend upon.

4.
Past the giant infant faces, we note the headset set, avoid Gauguin,
	a bastard, & linger on Degas, frightened by Van Gogh's
swollen streams, house beams bloated, fields of vitriol,

the presence pressing in. We follow the girls
	past Virgil & Dante, marble Byron, to Athena,
my childhood goddess, the skull-splitting mix

of strength & wisdom, a better warrior than War,
	to the Singer Sargent ceilings,
& the Bodhisattva of Compassion.

5.
I stand before her stone hands wishing
	for my daughters & each stony face
weathered into weakness, a ready fragment

to tender dust for peace. Before the sage,
	nothing myself, I glimpse the veil
of our trials, separations.

I cleave sorrow closer, leave it no room
	to escape & follow what passes
for the soul on to sameness.

For Frank Dalessio

*Computer Technician at Medford High School
who died from COVID*

Sometimes the light of my desktop would not
come on. The fan would spin, just pushing
dead air. The classics waited. You'd come, &
if there was life inside, you brought it back.
When it was doomed, you brought tools.

In the side of the library, you worked
happily for years. Skillful fingertips rough
from soldering. A mechanical room in triage,
each patient you would see to soon.

When I panicked, you'd hustle up the stairs, &
stayed after school. You didn't need
thanks. You smiled through fourteen years
of work many of us lamented, dreaming out
of small windows at trees that never saw
full sun. The last I saw you, masked,
when the district chose to open doors,
you set me up again, & I could teach.

Now, mornings begin as the small light
returns, & the whiteboard shines
words, black & clear as wisdom made
fresh by attention. How many learned
by the light you made come on
for all of us.

Something & Nothing

The great blue heron rises above the marshes,
landing on the elbow of a branch, extending the question
mark of its neck. It blends into the reeds & seems
to follow us. It is our honor to continue to see it
on this level. Jurassic Park is here, in Stow,
on the Assabet River. Flowers bloom on the surface,
watershield & lotus, content in their perfected
environment. Loosestrife teems & is poorly named.
Cattails lift their heads by bluebottles & turtles
puff watersmoke. We row morning together,

head for some coffee. Our friend leaves for a Zoom.
Her husband says, *Administration...they have nothing*
but think it's something. They call us all during Corona.
Says, *If they are on the phone, tell them it is summer,*
so we are on the river in our kayaks. If they keep talking?
Tell them I am in Bermuda, in the pool. If they ask,
What are you doing? *Tell them, I am looking at a cloud.*
Thirty minutes ago, I think I saw a horse in it.
But what if they say there is a meeting?
Ask, Do I have to be there?
If they say, no? *Tell them, fuck off.*

White Man's Overbite

Ellis asks me, *Is it fresh?* I say, *Yes,*
I see new lines clipped into a fade
& form from what they took away.

He's been in the studio, learning to layer
tracks, telling me, *There's levels*
to these bevels, so much good ish.

I confess I wore out "The Real Roxanne"
& "The King of Rock" on a Walkman & learned
how to tie the fat laces of my shell-toe ADIDAS
in 1985. That I carried a cardboard box
to breakdance at my Catholic school.

He's started drawing from his lyrical well
& is obsessed with Kendrick, so we talk
about where lines end & what power lies
in pausing. I tell him who Kunta Kinte was,
how where there's skill, there's jealousy, & why
one should read *Roots,* & that he should
be judicious when saying *bitch.*

Later, he sends a Soundcloud link
to a rap he's drafting, & again,
I cancel my fantasy of leaving the profession.

The Vulture

I tried to warn them, but from my beak
they would receive nothing. They saw baldness,
but that was adaptation. The building seethes
in the winter, freezes in the fall.
They took our committee for a wake,
pleasant voices for gospel,
but when it's drought, the wall writes itself.

From one who grieved her mother too long,
one for being gay, & one who couldn't skip
Bonnaroo, one Ivy who couldn't hack it,
one naive who drove girls home, one unkempt
who sat dutifully but too sour with his charges,
meals to pick clean. The feathers
of their affections: biographies, anthologies,
DVDs, tape rolls, ballpoints, ancillaries,
master texts I'd shadowed over, I digest
before they whet another veteran, &
let my brood have the marrow:
markers, copy paper; teach them
remnants of the habitat are fuel for
those who know the season's scarcities.

Shred the remainder without sentiment.
This is how the desert divides &
will again in August, as clean-winged
fledglings settle in to make a home of it.
Their dreaming will be my inheritance.

Our Parsons

My students no longer wonder how far a man will go
to curse his government, so they follow me
to Airstrip One, to the alcove where Winston takes
down the notebook he buys at the antique shop,
even hush when Julia fakes a fall to pass the note
telling Winston, *I love you,* & to meet in Victory Square.

They barely eye Charrington, before we study Snowden,
not suspecting the quiet proprietor in his frames,
more intrigued as to how one rents an apartment.
In the film, they'll be startled by Julia's ample fur—
& it won't surprise me that John Hurt as Winston
will not compel them; they prefer him as Ollivander,

saying, *The wand chooses the wizard.* On quizzes, they'll forget
who Syme is. His shrinking of the dictionary will seem
no dark magic. They will not agonize over a dying
language or fear a euphemism's gloved fist.
They'll see the lovers' age-gap as perversion, focus
on the prostitute Winston beds, his lipstick fetish,

the viscous gin, facecrime because it sounds like Facetime,
the sash of the Anti-Sex League, & wrap a plastic grief
around *the death of the orgasm.* They have only known *ownlife.*
They'll wince when O'Brien tears the tooth from our Last
Man, & reel, appropriately, at the rat-cage affixed
to his face. They'll want to know what a *prole* is.

They'll despise Parsons, his reeky sweat, his children
eager for hangings, but haven't met their neighbors they will
live beside who say they do not fear the helicopters
circling, the armored police taking the streets from protesters,
gunfire & separatist rhetoric, as much as unfamiliar faith.
They have not met the Parsons whose drains they'll dig

fingers into the grime for, share duties & meetings with,
wending through the calculated talk of the weather,
of our sporting wars, rations on special offer & the status quo.
They have not seen the defeated Parsons who is learning
empires depend on our attendance. They'll miss that Tom
chastised his young spies for their slingshot, that he screamed

out his last after embracing a world of austerity, betrayed
by himself & his children. Then they'll see the hollowness—
trained hatreds, safety in maxims, the facade
of orthodoxy that cracked in his sleeping chant, the living
sign of what change may come & what decency sleeps in such
people one still fears, more to be pitied than censored.

In Passing

For my student, Victor, who died young

Who was unimpressed but respected the work.
Who sat on the radiator beside his desk
to be closer to the sun. Allowed,
as he bothered no one.

Who played incandescent guitar for the class,
practiced hands let the music emerge
freed. Years past graduation, I saw him
on socials, his metal band in attractive rebellion,
hair flowing, tattoos, piercings, smokes,
photo comments a trail of inhabited joy.

A teacher wants to know them young, to believe
in their arc, to not damage or interfere.
To hear good news of them
from a proud periphery.

Keepers of the House

—The day the keepers of the house tremble and those that look out of
windows be darkened, because man goeth to his long home, and the
mourners go about the streets —Ecclesiastes 12:5

In his apron, Vincent plucks the vivid Italian cookies,
doubting correctly, *They're for my girls.*
He slaps his gut, *Nothing wrong with a sweet tooth.*
His name's tattooed elbow to wrist in cursive,
neck adorned by a thin gold
cross, telling me *the drugs* are why he left town,
Turning into Gloucester…poison just handed out to kids.

I hear you. I've read the epitaphs of morning texts,
learned the limits of a teacher's influence,
& haven't seen the last of the young shadows
like the one my colleague follows
home from school, trailing the specter
of powder & the silence of
a son, like the two ghosts in my classroom who return

to take their seats when I open the window for the breeze.
When they're listening, I preach, *Trust yourself, speak,*
don't court danger, but I'm talking to myself.
I regret I never told them that I used
to relish that back-tongue bitterness,
taking emptiness for oasis. Friends died,
but I was lucky. When I needed safety, I still had keys

to the house I couldn't wait to leave.

Attendance

All the mornings like burnt offerings,
raising smoke to entice fickle deities
but mainly wasting what a child
could do without. All my charges
dreaded numbered days—I kept pleasant
count. Especially in the testing rooms,
tucking laptops into sleepy carts,
I saw how futility usually dressed,
how any welcome is forgiveness
in a bad room, to never sit
if you want peace. Between lessons,

we traveled on the calendar, paid airlines
twice to do so. The sands were everything
we needed them to be. Then, we charted
nothing. We attended to the speeches
of our children. Between the months,
they grew, seismic. My love & I aged
into a calm, the kind no one calls romantic,
but peace is a transcendence
that isn't told as much as escapes
a record that tallies only absence.

Wyf Thinks of Summer

She spells it the old way, calls our girl a Viking
warrior, proclaims our halls safe, restores the day's
initial mystery, calls the sunny two-bed *Mexico*,
paints *All sorrow is less with bread* in our kitchen.
She makes a den of the ten-month year & bravely
brings them forth. She won't lie & say she doesn't
bask in the exhaust of the last bus, but once
vacation starts, it's slippery. Then August ads drop
the taunt of where we're all headed, friends
secretly pleased our lease's up & it's *the grind*
'til holidays give the pause no one challenges.
In December, when the chimney draws, she tends
the light down to the word's coals, plays Hestia
& lazes the interim of our state's cold spring,
but when June alights on the North Shore tides,
she wakes to chart them as they rise, inclines to
hear the salt-water music, not yet beginning to end.

In the Green Room

First on the call sheet, you make the coffee.
Morning's an aside, lightly delivered.
No line cues needed, we speak love, block the scene.
Your red car down-stages my black.
The street's overture of wheels on the hill
sends Ava to the bus, Stella screaming for a brush;
we are left to applaud ourselves.
Loafing in the green room, we re-read the scenes,
how we plan to play them today.
Costumes from the last performance flung
across chairs, the flooded calendar our old playbill,
makeup & hair product on the shared dresser,
practical props in our hands. No time to rest
in our roles, the curtain's coming up.

Acknowledgments

As One Does — *Misfit Magazine*

For the Student Who Fell Asleep
    During the Lesson on 9/11 — *Passengers Journal*

Dreamer — *Cultural Weekly*

Sophia — *Cimarron Review*

JiM "80" — *Panoplyzine*

Meadow Glen Mall — *Fourth &Sycamore*

A Child Says, *Morning* — *Panoplyzine*

Legend — *Panoplyzine*

Advisory — *Fourth & Sycamore*
& Alongside We Travel
(Autism Anthology)

Lockdown — *American Journal of Poetry*

On Hearing the Bomb Threat
    Was Not Intended for Us — *Chiron Review*

The Bodhisattva of Compassion — Nazim Hikmet Competition

For Frank Dalessio — *Chiron Review*

Something & Nothing — *Misfit Magazine*

White Man's Overbite — *Killer Whale Review*

The Vulture — *Panoplyzine*

Our Parsons — *Ithaca Review*

In Passing — *La Volpe*

Keepers of the House — *Nixes Mate*

Attendance — *Plainsongs*

Wyf Thinks of Summer — *Nixes Mate*

In the Green Room — *Ibbetson Street*

Dedication

To the teachers in my family: my mother, Rosemarie Heinegg, my mother-in-law, Carolyn Pfaffenbach, my late father, Peter, my wife, Wendy, and my sisters-in-law Jenny and Becky.

To my English department pals at Medford High School: Doug, Shawn, Eric, and Barry. To the poets who taught me: Jordan Smith, Kit Hathaway, and Robert Pinsky. To my favorite high school teacher, Tim Owens, who hooked me on Shakespeare by playing a great Lady Macbeth in class. To the memory of Bill Ziskin, who directed me as Mercutio in Romeo and Juliet at Linton High School. To the late Roy Williams who taught me science at SAAC in Schenectady, NY, and Pauline Walker at the Brooks-Hobbs in Medford, MA; they showed me teaching well was an art and an aspiration. To my Union College profs, especially Adrian Frazier, Misha Iossel, and the late Harry Marten, for encouraging my work. To the Boston University SED, where I got my MAT, and to Robert Oakes, my thoughtful mentor at Brighton High School. To teachers!

About the Author

photo by Stella Heinegg

Max Heinegg is the author of *Good Harbor* (2022), which won the inaugural Paul Nemser Prize from Lily Poetry Review Press, and *Going There* (2023).

Born in Cooperstown, NY, and raised in Schenectady, NY, he received his BA from Union College in 1995 and his MAT from Boston University in 1998. He has taught English in the Medford Public Schools since 1998.

His poems have been nominated for the Pushcart Prize and Best of the Net. He has won the Sidney Lanier Poetry Award, the Emily Stauffer Poetry Prize, and was a finalist for the poetry prizes of *Asheville Poetry Review, December Magazine, Crab Creek Review, Cultural Weekly, Rougarou Journal, Cutthroat Journal, Twyckenham Notes, West Virginia Writers*, and the Nazim Hikmet Prize.

His work has appeared in *32 Poems, The Cortland Review, Thrush, Nimrod,* and *The Night Heron Barks,* among others.

He is also a singer-songwriter whose records and adaptations of poems from the public domain can be heard at www.maxheinegg.com

He lives in Medford, MA where he is the 2025-2027 poet laureate of the city.

www.ingramcontent.com/pod-product-compliance
Lightning Source LLC
Chambersburg PA
CBHW030529130626
46549CB00007B/3157

* 9 7 8 1 9 5 7 7 5 5 4 8 9 *